Hugh Osgood

THE POWER OF PURITY

Maintaining a Christian testimony
in a compromising world

WWW.HUGHOSGOOD.COM

The Power of Purity:

Maintaining a Christian testimony in a compromising world
Copyright © 2016 by Hugh Osgood

Published by Charis House Publishing
St Paul's House
Edison Road
Bromley, BR2 0EP
contact@hughosgood.com

Scripture quotations, unless stated otherwise, are from the Holy Bible,
New King James Version, Copyright © 1979, 1980, 1982, 1988
Thomas Nelson Inc.
Published by Thomas Nelson Publishers

ISBN 978-0-9935488-0-2

Contents

Introduction   5

1. The source of purity   9

2. Securing purity   31

3. Safeguarding our purity   59

Contents

Introduction

1. ... ...

2. ... ... party

3. Safeguarding our part

Introduction

This book began life as a three-session teaching conference where we considered purity in the context of God's nature and the nature of fallen humanity. So it is more than just a practical handbook on Christian living.

The first chapter makes us think of God with awe and wonder. The second chapter faces the realities of human nature and the appropriateness of God's redemption. Together these prepare us for the more practical aspects of expressing the purity of God in our daily lives.

Given its structure this book should prove to be a stimulating and rewarding read for you. Our lives change for the better as we come to see things more clearly.

I trust this book helps you in your ever-growing relationship with our utterly pure and endlessly gracious God.

Hugh Osgood

1

The source of purity

The source of purity

The source of purity

I was a little hesitant about calling this book the 'The Power of Purity' as I could imagine someone saying "If I become pure, I'll have the power to impress everybody." For me, that is the complete opposite of purity. Seeking personal power always compromises purity.

In the Sermon on the Mount Jesus said *'Let your light so shine before men, that they may see your good works and glorify your Father in heaven'*.[1] The light that we are able to shine, and the good works we are able to do, are all drawn from God's goodness, which is why He receives the glory. There is no glory for those who try to mount their own personal purity parade. We are to live aright to the glory of God.

There is, however, a power that can bring purity to our lives, and surely that is what we need when the pressure to compromise is all around us. We find that pressure in our workplaces, communities, schools and colleges, even

[1] Matthew 5:16.

in our churches and families. We need the power of God to sustain us under such pressure and the good news is that the power of God's purity is strong enough to do just that; it can make us pure and keep us pure.

So, having acknowledged that the source of our purity is God Himself, we need to backtrack to before creation, to the point where, *'In the beginning was the Word, and the Word was with God, and the Word was God'*.[2] Understanding the essence of God's eternal purity will help us appreciate the way He makes it available to us in Christ.

There was never a time when Jesus was not. When the psalmist recorded God the Father as saying, *'Today I have begotten You'*,[3] there was no timescale being placed on the begetting. *'Today'* highlighted a celebration of an existing reality, and when the psalm is quoted in the New Testament by the writer to the Hebrews, the Son's eternal right to rule and reign is affirmed by linking the *'today'* with the reality of Christ's resurrection.[4] Similar criteria apply when defining the Son as *'begotten'* (or more fully, in New Testament terminology, *'the only begotten…'*[5]). It was a confirmation of His uniqueness, role and positioning

---

[2] John 1:1.

[3] Psalm 2:7.

[4] Hebrews 1:1-5.

[5] John 3:16.

within the Godhead. The truth is set down for us in Psalm 90:2, '*From everlasting to everlasting You are God*', a statement that applies equally to Father, Son and Holy Spirit. Neither the Holy Spirit nor the Son has ever done anything other than act in perfect unity with the Father.[6]

When we begin to look more closely at God in His pre-creation eternal presence, we see purity in every aspect of His triune existence. When the Bible defines God as light, it is pure light – '*God is light and in Him is no darkness at all*'.[7] When the Bible defines God as love,[8] His love is absolutely pure and without imperfection. When the Bible defines God as life itself,[9] it is, as Jesus confirmed, life in all its fullness. So before God created anything, He, the God who is light, love and life, existed in absolute purity.

The dwelling place of God

In writing to Timothy, the apostle Paul urged Timothy to '*pursue righteousness, goodness, faith, love, patience, gentleness*', yet the very same passage speaks of God as

---

[6] Genesis 1:2.
[7] 1 John 1:5.
[8] 1 John 4:8.
[9] John 14:6.

'dwelling in unapproachable light'.[10] So how do we approach
the unapproachable? It seems that even when we lay aside
all that is negative in our lives and pursue the highest
standards of living, our purity still falls short of God's
spotlessness.

Whilst this may appear discouraging, it is important
to be realistic. God is light and the light that emanates
from God provides the environment in which He lives.
He needs no other space in which to exist. There is an
aura of glory around Him. It is the *Shekinah* glory of His
presence. God dwells in the brightness of His own light.
Seeing the utter perfection of God's purity rightly makes
us hesitate to step into such blazing glory. So it is better
by far to acknowledge that we can only enter in because
God invites us than to live in the realms of pointless naïve
presumption.

No-one has seen God in all His fullness. Jesus came
to make Him known and one day we are going to see Him
as He is.[11] That is going to be incredible. We are going to
see God's purity in all its spectacular glory. Right now,
though, there can be anticipation in our hearts… and it can

---

[10]   1 Timothy 6:11-16.
[11]   John 1:18.

be an inspirational anticipation and not a condemnatory one.[12]

As we grasp more of God's purity, the sheer glory of it attracts us rather than repels us. Just as a moth always goes to the light, and often seals its own destruction in doing so, so there is something in us that is drawn to God's blazing purity, even though we sense it will eventually cost us every atom of our self-centredness.

In going back before the creation we find God at rest in Himself, dwelling in perfect contentment. Contrary to some people's suggestions, God never has been subject to loneliness, nor felt obliged to create because of a lack of companionship. Clearly love does need a focus but love is at the very centre of God's nature and therefore comes before all His creative acts.

Some people say they have a problem understanding the Trinity. Actually, I would have a problem understanding God if there were no Trinity. Love does not exist without an object. God is love because God the Father loves the Son and the Holy Spirit; God the Holy Spirit loves the Father and the Son; and God the Son loves the Father and the Holy Spirit. God did not become Love when He created,

---

[12]   1 John 3:1-3.

nor did He create us out of frustrated affection. He has always been and will always be Love.

Actually, I believe the reason God made us is because He is creative and His capacity for showing His light, life and love is immeasurable. The Bible opens with the words *'In the beginning God created'*.[13] In fact, it is worth pausing after the first four words and reflecting on their simplicity – *'In the beginning God'*. Those who ask "Who invented God?" have to accept that if someone had invented God, they would be facing the same question, but over another creator. The very definition of God is that He is without beginning and without end. He is Life.

When Moses asked God His name, God replied 'I am that I am', which also includes 'I was what I was', and 'I will be what I will be'. From everlasting to everlasting, He is! We cannot discern a starting point and we cannot ascribe a finishing point. He is the Alpha and Omega, the One Who invented time.

In creating, God was giving expression to Himself, creating purity out of His purity. Before forming heaven and earth He had created an angelic order to offer pure worship and to exemplify purely-motivated servant-heartedness. There was nothing selfish in God creating

[13] Genesis 1:1.

such a worshipping company; its ultimate role would lie in serving us as the creation yet to come, and in inspiring us in our worship.

Furthermore, just as God revels in mutual love, so He rejoices in mutual honour. God the Son delights to see the Father enthroned in worship, God the Father is thrilled to see the same for His Son, and God the Holy Spirit enthuses when the Father and Son are both so honoured, knowing that He is equally honoured by them.

As we envisage angelic worshippers encircling the throne crying *'Holy, Holy, Holy'* in acknowledgement of our triune God's ever-consistent purity, we gain a glimpse into the very heart of that blaze of pure light, which is the dwelling place of God.

The creativity of God

When God created, He made everything external to Himself. If the angels, which He made first, had been part of His being, the rebellion in their ranks, which tragically did occur, would have compromised the truth that *'God is light and in Him is no darkness at all'*.[14]

---

[14] 1 John 1:5.

Significantly, though, an external creation need not be a distant creation. The apostle Paul acknowledged this when he spoke to the Athenians at the Areopagus. He used the words of a Greek poet to declare, *'in Him we live and move and have our being'*.[15] So God's presence is all-pervasive. He has not wound up His creation as if it were a clockwork system to be sent spinning into space unattended. He is *'upholding all things by the word of His power'*.[16] God's omnipresence facilitates His close commitment to all that He has created. And it is this commitment that guarantees the ultimate triumph of His purity over the blight introduced by an angelic rebellion.

But we need to bring the issue of purity more firmly down to earth, both literally and figuratively. Creating a perfect world in the wake of an angelic rebellion could be said to have carried risks for God, especially as the crown of that new creation was to be given a foundational choice. In a safe environment a choice between closer dependence on the Creator and greater independence from the Creator would have been a relatively straightforward test. However, with rebellion in the air, the consequences of giving such a choice took on an awesome seriousness to the point where clear warnings had to be in place for the choice to proceed.

---

[15] Acts 17:28.

[16] Hebrews 1:3.

To carry weight the test still had to be voluntary, but everything changed once 'greater independence' became unavoidably entangled with an existing spirit of rebellion. Set in the starkest terms the choice had become: 'opt for greater dependence and experience more of God's pure liberty, love, light and life'; or 'opt for greater independence and experience the taint of enslavement, discord, darkness and death'.

Clear warnings, however, were not the only thing God had in place before continuing with the test. In His wisdom, He had ensured that a wrong choice would not ultimately mark the end. After much preparatory work the choice could be re-established. Purity could be back, with God Himself coming as the Light in the midst of our darkness, walking our streets and dispensing His liberty, love and life.

But before we get ahead of ourselves, let us pause and consider the light that, according to the opening of John's Gospel, gives *'light to every man coming into the world'.*[17] John's description presents a light that is individually relevant and yet universally applied. It is the Light that John the Baptist was able to point to when preparing the way for Jesus: *'John… was not that Light, but was sent to bear witness of that Light. That was the true Light which gives*

---

[17] John 1:9.

light to every man coming into the world.[18] Punctuated in this way, it sounds as if every person who has ever lived (and whoever will live) has, from the moment of birth, an awareness of something beyond his or herself.[19] The concept of a universally granted measure of light has to be handled with care.

Some speak of such a measure as the light that dawns on a living creation so it can acknowledge a life-giving Creator. Others believe it is physical life itself, loaned until it returns to the Life-giver.[20] 'Loaned life' theorists, however, have to ensure that they do not distort the link between physical and spiritual life, giving the impression that the whole of humanity will always be left lifeless in the face of eternity, deprived even of the opportunity to stand before God's throne and bow in acceptance of His justice.

The words of Ecclesiastes 3:11 helpfully link present and future in setting out both the purpose and the limitations of this universally experienced light: *'He has made everything beautiful in its time. Also He has put eternity in*

---

[18] John 1:6,8,9.

[19] The NIV and some other versions link the *'coming into the world'* with the *'Light'* rather than with *'every man'*. Hence, *'The true light that gives light to every man was coming into the world'*. John 1:9 NIV.

[20] Ecclesiastes 11:7.

their hearts, except that no-one can find out the works God does from beginning to end'. It is a light that launches a glorious quest without guaranteeing a glorious conclusion, unless further light is shed along the way.

Many agree that this light, which is given to every man, is best understood in terms of our conscience. Every person in the world – no matter who they are or whether or not they have heard the Gospel – has some inner awareness of right and wrong. It is, of course, far from infallible and can become badly twisted. Nonetheless it does provide a kind of internal regulation, serving as a pointer to the true righteousness that is only found through accepting God's light and life in Christ.

It is part of the wonder of God's creativity, love and mercy that, despite the high price humanity rightly had to pay for disregarding His warnings and rejecting a God-engaged future, God has not left us without a witness to His purity and presence.

The redemptive grace of God

When Jesus came, He brought with Him the glory of God:

> *And the Word became flesh and dwelt amongst us,*
> *and we beheld His glory, the glory as of the only*
> *begotten of the Father, full of grace and truth.[21]*

Within the Godhead there is light, love and life, and there is also grace and truth. Some joke that the slowest thing on four legs is two Christians trying to go through a door - "After you." "No, after you." "No, after you." – but in a way that is grace in operation. Grace thrives when self-interest is set aside. As the Father defers to the Son and the Holy Spirit, and the Holy Spirit and the Son defer to the Father, we see the marks of eternal grace. There is no self-aggrandisement in the Godhead. Jesus took on humanity so that He could serve us and bring us into His Father's plan.

We have already touched briefly on Genesis 1:1. In the remainder of this chapter we will consider Genesis chapters 2 and 3, taking the text literally so as to establish principles that lie beyond the recorded incidents. In Genesis 1 we

---

[21] John 1:14.

have an overview of how God progressively populated the earth. In Genesis 2 we have a close-up, showing God's provision of an environment for humanity. In Genesis 3 we see the consequences of humanity's early actions.

Life and relationship go hand-in-hand. Coals burn well alongside each other in a fire but a coal on its own soon grows cold. Human life was designed to be lived in relationship with God; from the moment the first man and woman stood on the earth they had a sufficient measure of God's life within them to establish a relationship with Him, since God had said *'Let us'* (and it is plural) *'make man in our image'*.[22] Importantly, an even greater measure of life and relationship with Him was there to be voluntarily entered into through the tree of life that He had placed in the middle of their garden.

Of course, God could have acted differently. He could have put all of His life, both physical and spiritual, into humanity from the outset, but He purposed instead to make the fullness of life subject to choice. Furthermore, He decided to highlight that choice by providing an alternative option. Setting the tree of the knowledge of good and evil alongside the tree of life ensured that it would not be just a 'take it or leave it' decision.

---

[22] Genesis 1:26.

Now it is theoretically possible that, if it had not been for the rebellion in heaven, the second tree could simply have been a tree of knowledge. That would still have made the basic point that life can either be lived in closer relationship with God or through greater dependence on our human wits and wisdom. However, the rebellion in the angelic order meant that there was now a negative side to knowledge, with evil available to be known alongside the good.

The warnings God gave to guide the decision could not have been clearer, *'Of every tree of the garden you may freely eat; but of the tree of the knowledge of good and evil you shall not eat, for in the day you eat of it you shall die'.*[23] In other words, "You can choose, but if you choose this particular one, you will be rebelling against my wishes."

Not surprisingly, the tree of the knowledge of good and evil held a fascination for the leading rebellious angel. In coming to the woman in the form of a serpent, he was quick to promote his preferred tree by saying, *'You will not surely die. For God knows that in the day you eat of it your eyes will be opened, and you will be like God, knowing good and evil.'*[24] In reality, he could not have been more wrong. In

---

[23] Genesis 2:16,17

[24] Genesis 3:4-5.

the day the fruit was eaten, death would enter the earth and evil would lodge in the eater's heart in a way that God had never known, and will never personally experience, for, whilst God sees evil externally, the eater would know it internally.

Arguably God could have fenced off the fateful tree, but that would doubtless have engendered yet more superstition. As it was, by the time Eve was having her conversation with the serpent she was saying, *'God has said, "You shall not eat it, nor shall you touch it, lest you die"',*[25] when in fact there was no such embargo. If Adam and Eve had wished, they could have carved their names in the bark and it would not have made the slightest difference. Sometimes when embargoes, even supposed embargoes, are enforced, superstition increases and the temptation level rises. The only issue was eating, and with two trees in the middle of the garden, one with a prohibition on it and one without, God could not have given a stronger indication - He wanted humanity to have the benefit of constantly feasting from the tree of life and living in an even closer relationship with Him.

Tragically, humanity lost so much the day that the first man and woman ate from the tree of the knowledge of

---

[25] Genesis 3:3.

good and evil. Something died on the inside of them. They still had a conscience, but their conscience was seared. They still had contact with God, but their openness with Him had been marred. They still had a relationship with each other but that too had changed. They now saw each other's nakedness, as the glory of God's covering had gone from their lives.

But what of the opportunity to discover the fullness of life that lay beyond the innocence of Eden? We know that God always intended something better for humanity than innocence; that is why He introduced the tree of life. He certainly had no wish to burden humanity with the consequences of eating from the tree of the knowledge of good and evil. His desire has always been to have us share in the preciousness of His purity, a purity that is not just the absence of sin but is the highest expression of His light, love and life.

Once impurity had become part of humanity's internal experience, the tree of life, the access point to God's ultimate purity, had to be placed out of reach until a transformative approach had been established for those genuinely seeking its benefits. Furthermore, as the consequences of the first man and woman's ill-considered decision began to be felt throughout the whole created order, a whole global recovery programme also needed to be brought into play. Everything that had been fashioned free from death, decay and disaster was now beginning to groan under the weight of fragility and fruitlessness.

It seems ironic that before their unceremonious expulsion from the garden the first man, Adam, should have looked on the first woman, his wife, and named her Eve, *'the mother of all living'*,[26] since death had already taken hold. Initially death had confronted them as a disconnection from God, but a physical outworking of death was about to become evident.[27] The couple's firstborn became a murderer and their second-born his victim.[28] Maybe it was the words of rebuke that Adam had just heard God speak to the rebellious angel, the seducing serpent, back there in the garden that had inspired him in his naming. Hearing God tell the devil that a day would come when he would be crushed by One from among the woman's offspring may have prompted Adam's optimism.[29] If Adam had truly realised it, he had just heard the words of redemption that would set the tone for every age to come whereby life in all its fullness would be accessible to all humanity.

---

[26] Genesis 3:20.
[27] Genesis 3:8,9.
[28] Genesis 4:8.
[29] Revelation 20:2 and Genesis 3:15.

When Adam and Eve were driven out of Eden, God set an angelic being with a flaming sword to guard the way to the tree of life.[30] It was as if God were adding another redemptive picture, one that was saying 'the journey to the tree of life will cost you that self-centred existence which you have chosen to be your life experience'. There needs to be purification in order to touch purity.

Of course, they knew such a journey was beyond them, as did King David when he said many centuries later, using different imagery: *'Who may ascend into the hill of the Lord? Or who may stand in His holy place? He who has clean hands and a pure heart...'*[31] The agreement within the Godhead, made even before the dust of the earth from which Adam and Eve were fashioned had itself been formed, was being set in motion. God the Son would come Himself as the promised Offspring and in His purity experience the cut of the flaming sword to open the way for us to stand in God's holy place.[32]

---

[30] Genesis 3:24.

[31] Psalm 24:3,4.

[32] Hebrews 10:19, 20 makes a similar point using the post-Eden symoblism of a ripped Temple veil.

And so to the first sign of h

Just nine generations after Adam and Eve we discover the first real sign of hope. At first sight the situation looked anything but promising. Wickedness had increased in those nine generations and life was tough. Apart from a now inaccessible garden of perfection, the ground worldwide was as hard as iron as a consequence of humanity's rebellion, and growing crops was all but impossible.[33] Prophetically, a man named Lamech called his baby boy 'Noah', which means comfort, saying *'This one will comfort us concerning the work and the toil of our hands, because of the ground which the Lord has cursed'*.[34] It did not seem comforting when the fountains of the deep were broken up and the windows of heaven were opened, but when the flood was over and the waters subsided, the earth was transformed.[35] Things could grow in a way that was not possible before.

And where was the tree of life? It had been shifted from a geographical location to a place in the eternal purposes of God. The tree of life is no longer tied to the ancient past or limited to a fertile Mesopotamian plain.

[33] Genesis 3:17-19.
[34] Genesis 5:29.
[35] Genesis 7:11; 9:20.

book of Revelation speaks of the tree of life being the Paradise of God.[36] For a few hours, at the centre point of human history, a cross was planted on a Judean hillside so that the Son of God could be nailed there for us, defeating death, darkness and disorder and bringing life and love to light. The tree that put death to death in the midst of a Middle-Eastern day and the tree of life in the Paradise of God are one and the same. Redemption is rooted in history and is open to all who come via the cross to the dwelling place of God. The source of our purity lies at the heart of God's purity, a purity evidenced in God's uncompromising givenness to His creation.

---

[36] Revelation 2:7.

2

Securing purity

Securing purity

We have seen how the types and figures of Genesis 2 and 3 find their fulfilment in Jesus: He is the promised Offspring who suffered the bruising of His heel, His sacrifice can be seen as the journey through the flaming sword and His cross now stands as the tree of life. Yet the Old Testament sets out many more 'object lessons' that Jesus has fulfilled and some of these will help us as we look at securing purity.

As a framework, I will take three words found in 1 John 5:8: '*And there are three that bear witness on earth: the Spirit, the water and the blood; and these three agree as one.*' The key words are the Spirit, the water and the blood, so let us consider each, in reverse order, under the headings 'a price to pay', 'a cleansing required' and 'a conviction needed'.

A price to pay

It could be said that, despite their attempts to shift the blame, all three parties involved in the Genesis 3 garden incident – Adam, Eve and the serpent – had to pay a price. When Adam was confronted, he blamed Eve and God, yet paid a price in terms of the barrenness of the ground. When Eve was confronted, she blamed the serpent, yet the pain of childbearing came her way. When the serpent was confronted, he admitted no guilt, yet was consigned to the dust. But in the midst of this there was hope; once the serpent was cast to the ground, he was rendered right for trampling on, and it was to be the Seed of the woman who would do it.

> *The Lord God said to the serpent: "Because you have done this, you are cursed more than all cattle, and more than every beast of the field; on your belly you shall go, and you shall eat dust all the days of your life. And I will put enmity between you and the woman, and between your seed and her Seed; He shall bruise your head, and you shall bruise His heel."* [1]

---

[1] Genesis 3:14.

The Seed of the woman, although an Innocent Party who had contributed nothing to the disobedience in the garden, was destined to pay a high price indeed to ensure the serpent's ultimate downfall.

The bruising of the Seed's heel was to be a traumatic event with cosmic significance. When the final book of the Bible describes Jesus as '*the Lamb slain from the foundation of the world*', [2] it confirms that His willingness to lay down His life, declared at the outset of creation, secured our redemptive hope. It is a poignant commitment made in the face of a recent angelic revolt and with an awareness that a then soon-to-be-created humanity would make a rebellious choice. The statement uses the language of sacrifice, terminology we will need to understand if we are to grasp the significance of the blood securing God's purity for us.

The first physical death implied in the Bible was actually a sacrificial one. An animal gave its life so that Adam and Eve could be clothed with skin rather than with leaves.[3] They needed to be taught a lesson in the costliness of redemption. Leaves were cheap but ineffective. Setting things right in a world marred by sin was going to demand far more than they could imagine.

---

[2] Revelation 13:8.
[3] Genesis 3:21.

As God had given them dominion over the created world, their fall not only resulted in disorder and death for them but brought decay into the whole of creation. In time their God-given dominion would turn into self-centred domination, with oppression replacing care. Humans would be taking advantage of each other's newly-perceived vulnerabilities in order to lord it over one another. The concept of sacrifice to cover human vulnerability was clearly going to be of real importance. However, many other facets of sacrifice would need to be understood in the unfolding of God's plan for recovery.

Interestingly, Noah, Abraham and Job were no strangers to animal sacrifice.   Noah sacrificed as a thanksgiving to God after the flood, whilst Abraham and Job saw sacrifices as a way of securing God's favour.[4] Fortunately, God lifted Abraham's understanding to a higher level when He showed Him that His favour is secured when sacrifice is understood in the context of substitutionary intervention. As Abraham had his knife raised over his son Isaac, God stepped in and provided a ram for the offering. As the nations around Abraham sacrificed their children, he discovered that in God's heart sacrifice and substitution go hand-in-hand.

---

[4] Genesis 8:21; 12:8; Job 1:5.

The principle of 'the God who provides' then took on far wider prominence when Moses established the priesthood. Now a whole nation could come to see that *'without the shedding of blood there is no remission of sins'.* It was a lesson in sacrifice and substitution that took on greater meaning given the Jewish understanding that the *'the life is in the blood'.*[5] Under the Law of Moses, knowing that life had to be given for sin meant that everyone bringing a sacrifice for sin had a personal appreciation of God's mercy. This heightened the reality of each individual's sense of forgiveness, foreshadowing the even greater revelation of God's grace and purity that was to come.

Paul's letter to the Romans is particularly helpful here since, along with the letter to the Hebrews, it sheds light on Old Testament practices. In it Paul develops an argument for God's justice by stating that *'the wages of sin is death, but the gift of God is eternal life in Christ Jesus our Lord'.*[6] He explains that the rebellious decision at the outset of human history, which has left death endemic, has to be set alongside the reality that what the first humans did we all would have done too. His assertion is that we have all been proving this on a regular basis by making

---

[5] Hebrews 9:22; Leviticus 17:11.

[6] Romans 6:23.

our own wayward decisions, hence his statement, *'For all have sinned and fall short of the glory of God'.*[7]

So in returning to our Genesis 3:15 understanding, the bruising of the Offspring's heel had to include death in order to bring a just restoration. When Adam and Eve sinned and discovered straight away that something had died on the inside of them, it was only the first step in the unfolding of God's justice. Sin is no light matter and death has many facets. A bruising may sound less momentous than a crushing, but we need to keep our thinking on track. It is true that a mortal wound was to be inflicted on the serpent from which he would never recover, but Jesus had to endure death on behalf of every one of us, and, in triumphing over death in His resurrection, He opened up the way to life for all who put their trust in Him.[8]

It is at this point that we can see the pattern whereby an initial representative's wilful error can be rectified by a subsequent Representative's right decision. When Adam made his disastrous choice he was acting on behalf of the whole of humanity and his decision has since affected every one of us. The good news is that what one man lost for all, one Man can regain for all. Our own sinful actions leave us deserving death, but the Son of God has come in

---

[7] Romans 3:23.

[8] Hebrews 2:9.

the flesh as our Representative, and His righteous action pays the price for each of us once for all.[9] No wonder the New Testament describes Jesus as both the last Adam and the second Man, names that signify the end of a corrupted order and herald the re-introduction of God's original plan.

The incredible costliness of the death Jesus experienced for us is clear from His cry on the cross, '*My God, my God why have You forsaken Me?*'[10] As He, in His spotlessness, became a sin offering for us and carried the weight of humanity's rebellion, He experienced a separation. It differed from the separation experienced by Adam, not least in the fact that when Adam lost his connectedness it was God who came looking, saying, 'Adam, where are you?'.[11] When the last Adam, Jesus, the second Man, felt the pain of separation He instantly called out to His Father, longing for the connection to be restored, not just for Himself, which was a given, but for every one of us who is prepared to receive His salvation.

In paying the price on the cross, Jesus was crushing the serpent's head through the bruising of His own heel. He was also shedding His blood in a way that was prefigured

---

[9]   Hebrews 10:10.
[10] Matthew 27:46. Mark 15:34.
[11] Genesis 3:9.

by many Old Testament types. Different sectors of the Church now have their own ways of talking about the blood of Jesus. Some speak of being 'washed in the blood' whilst others talk of drawing 'blood lines' or 'pleading the blood'. There is an understandable desire to pick up figuratively on the way the Israelites placed blood on their lintels to protect their homes as part of God's requirements on that fateful last night in Egypt when they had to eat a roasted lamb before setting out on their journey.[12]

Ultimately, of course, our destiny is determined by our acceptance of the One who laid down His life for us. The cross not only provided blood for protection but also opened up a pathway to purity by cleansing us from sin and renewing our relationship with the God of light, love and life.

Our 1 John 5:8 Bible verse tells us that the Spirit is in agreement with the blood, and, given that the context of the verse relates specifically to the person of Jesus and the nature of His ministry, it seems appropriate to follow some later biblical texts and see the Word alongside this unity of blood, water and Spirit:

For there are three that bear witness in heaven: the Father, the Word, and the Holy Spirit; and these

[12]   Exodus 12:3-13.

> *three are one. And there are three that bear witness*
> *on earth: the Spirit, the water, and the blood; and*
> *these three agree as one.*[13]

At creation the Spirit of God moved on the face of the deep as God the Father spoke His word. The Holy Spirit then took the word and brought it into being.

We are told in Hebrews 12:24 that *'the blood of Jesus speaks better things than that of Abel'*. When Abel, the second son of Adam and Eve, was killed by his brother, his blood cried out for vengeance. Jesus' blood cries out for our forgiveness and the Holy Spirit is able to work with that cry to bring that forgiveness into our lives. God's forgiveness is always complete: *'As far as the east is from the west, so far has He removed our transgressions from us'.*[14] *'If we confess our sins, He is faithful and just to forgive us our sins and to cleanse us from all unrighteousness.'*[15] Our purity is that important to Him.

In God's eyes the person who has been forgiven is as spotless as the one who has never sinned. Taking hold of God's forgiveness is a major factor in breaking what to us

---

[13] 1 John 5:7,8. Note: the NIV (and some other versions, following earlier manuscripts) omit the words from *'in heaven'* (v7) through to *'on earth'* (v8).

[14] Psalm 103:12.

[15] 1 John 1:9.

seem to be persistent sin cycles in our lives. We need to be saying to ourselves '*how much more shall the blood of Christ, who through the eternal Spirit offered Himself without sin to God, cleanse your conscience from dead works to serve the living God?*'[16] Seeing the dead weight of guilt lift off our lives enables us to be set free and to live with renewed hope.

There are two different Greek words used for 'pure' in the New Testament. One, *hagnos*, has its roots in the word for 'holiness' and carries the sense of 'separation from' and 'separation unto'. Purity does not come simply through a separation from sin. We begin to discover purity when we are separated unto the One who is absolutely pure. The other word, *katharos*, has the same root as 'cathartic' and is to do with cleansing. 1 John 1:7 is very specific: '*The blood of Jesus cleanses us from all sin*'. We are made clean and set apart so that we can live in relationship with the One who is purity itself.

A cleansing required

Having looked at cleansing by the blood, we now need to take the concept of cleansing further by looking at the second part of our 1 John 5:8 threefold agreement, the water.

---

[16]   Hebrews 9:14.

In Ephesians 5:26 we are told that Christ has sanctified (set apart) and cleansed the Church *'with the washing of water by the word'* and in John 15:3 we have Jesus Himself saying *'You are already clean because of the word which I have spoken to you'*. So we cannot overlook the Word of God when it comes to being washed and made clean.

Jesus made His 'cleansed by the word' statement when likening Himself to a vine with His disciples as the branches. He was in effect telling the twelve that they had already been pruned by His spoken word and that maintaining their unity with Him, whilst accepting further pruning from His Father, was the way to greatest fruitfulness. It is an important metaphor to consider when looking at the power of God's word to purify us.

In the Garden of Eden, Eve was attracted to the fruit because of three things: it seemed good for food (*'the lust of the flesh'*), it looked good (*'the lust of the eyes'*), and it would make her wise (*'the pride of life'*). These hooks, which are labelled in 1 John 2:16 as *'all that is in the world'*, are the very same inward pulls that have troubled humanity ever since. They pressurise us inwardly through the flesh; they pressurise us outwardly through the world; and they pressurise us through the seduction of the devil. Three problems coming at us from three angles! The cross deals with all three but it is the effectiveness of God's Word in dealing with the flesh that we need to consider here.

We can begin by asking ourselves how it was that, when Adam and Eve ate the forbidden fruit and something in them died, they did not drop lifeless to the ground. There must have been something that kept them going. Somehow, separated from God, but fortified by the fruit of the tree of the knowledge of good and evil, they used their physical frame and God-given mental and emotional resources to drive them onwards. Their eyes had been open to the potential of their physicality, intellect and personality and their desires and aspirations caused the potential to develop rapidly, unchecked by the now absent spiritual element that had once made Adam and Eve distinct. Godly balance had been lost, and ever since, as Paul teaches in Ephesians 2:1, humanity has been '*dead in trespasses and sins*' forcing onwards in the strength of our over-inflated flesh, until we come to life in Christ.

As we look back at our own lives we can see how we ourselves survived before we were born again. We ate our meals. We dressed ourselves each morning. We went through school. We probably secured a job. We may even have managed to convince someone that we were worth marrying. And we did all of this whilst, as the Bible says, we were dead in trespasses and sins. So there was something that was pushing us forward: it was the lust of the flesh, the lust of the eyes and the pride of life.

Humanity is good at making a virtue of the things that are actually our problem. We could say that it is everyone's desire to impress that keeps the world going round. In a sense, it is the pride of life that motivates us all until we find freedom from it in Christ. The Bible says that *'where envy and self-seeking exist, confusion and every evil thing will be there'*.[17] If this world is to be freed from evil and confusion, all our overgrown desires need surgery. 'Self' needs cutting back. 'Self' received a death blow when we came to Christ for salvation but now Christ comes to us again and again saying, "Still too much flesh." We have to decrease so that He might increase.

In the Old Testament, God's people had a physical illustration. Every time a boy was born, an outward mark of circumcision was made on his body. It was a pointer to the bigger mark God longed to make on the inside of all His people, cutting everyone back at the very centre of their beings to bring everything into balance. Circumcision of the heart has always been part of God's recovery plan for all.[18] And the word of God can serve as the knife: *'For*

---

[17] James 3:16.
[18] Deuteronomy 10:16.

the word of God is living and powerful, and sharper than any two-edged sword, piercing even to the division of soul and spirit, and of joints and marrow, and is a discerner of the thoughts and intents of the heart'.[19]

The twelve had been with Jesus for three years when He told them, '*You are already clean because of the word which I have spoken to you'*. All kinds of words had been spoken to them and every word had impacted them. When James and John requested the seats in heaven at the left-hand and right-hand of Jesus, they were told, '*Whoever desires to be great among you shall be your servant.*'[20] It was a transformative word and a very deliberate knife-cut.

The prophecy that Simeon gave to Mary when she presented the infant Jesus in the Temple, makes it even plainer: '*a sword will pierce through your own soul also'*.[21] Thirty-three years later Mary was standing before the cross, looking at her Son with love and concern. Jesus then spoke directly to her and to John alongside her. His words were '*sharper than any two-edged sword'* and cut cleanly into her heart: '*Woman, behold your son!'* and to John, '*Behold your mother!'*[22] It was a painful but necessary severance.

---

[19] Hebrews 4:12.
[20] Mark 10:35-45.
[21] Luke 2:35.
[22] John 19:26,27.

Jesus was looking ahead, beyond His death and resurrection, to His ascension and the outpouring of the Spirit. He wanted Mary to experience the greater closeness with Him that this would bring. He knew that even her natural maternal feelings could undermine the intimacy that would be available to all who would come to Him through faith. Having Christ within her spiritually through the power of the Spirit had to surpass the physical indwelling she had experienced in her pregnancy.

The cut of God's Word is something that should never be despised. But we need to return to the connection between the water and the Word; we are helped by the fact that on the night Jesus told His disciples that they were already clean through His Word, He also washed their feet.

Peter's response to the foot-washing was typically forthright. Peter said to Him, *'Lord, are You washing my feet?' Jesus answered and said to him, 'What I am doing you do not understand now, but you will know after this'*. The conversation continued as Peter said to Him, *'You shall never wash my feet'* and Jesus replied, *'If I do not wash you, you have no part with Me'*. Simon Peter then said to Him, *'Lord, not my feet only, but also my hands and my head'* to which Jesus replied, '*He who is bathed needs only to wash his feet, but is completely clean*'. [23]

We may think that our heads and hands need repeated washing but it is actually our feet that pick up the dust; unless, that is, we see ourselves as some kind of superior Christian, exempt from walking in the world. Having pristine feet, though, does not give us the right to say to others "If you had as much faith as I have, those challenges you face would never have come your way." Remember it is those who are prepared to march into the devil's territory who are more likely to pick up the dust of the battlefield and suffer the scars and bruises of warfare.

Maybe it was a suspicion that I might have received some bruises that once prompted someone to obey Jesus' injunction and come to wash my feet.[24] I found it really humbling and in truth I was embarrassed by the love and care. It made me realise that Jesus was not washing the disciples' feet because the host of the house might have overlooked it. Jesus wanted to show them the heart of true service. Titus 3:4-6 makes a similar link between washing and care:

---

[23] John 13:6-10.
[24] John 13:14.

But when the kindness and the love of G
Saviour toward man appeared, not by w...
righteousness which we have done, but according
to His mercy He saved us, through the washing of
regeneration and renewing of the Holy Spirit, whom
He poured out on us abundantly through Jesus
Christ, our Saviour.

Jesus took on our humanity and came among us, full of grace and truth, to bring the purity of God to earth. He did not come to taunt us with unattainable goals but to change us so that we could become partakers of the divine nature. The cross had to be more than an inspiration for all who suffer, or even a means of crushing the devil. The restoration of humanity has always been the major theme on God's heart.

When we first come to Christ we need to be thoroughly washed – our heads for our thoughts, our hearts for our intentions, our hands for our actions and our feet for our journeyings. The effectiveness of this initial washing is clear from 1 Corinthians 6:11 where Paul, having given a list of those who will not inherit the kingdom of God, says, *'And such were some of you'*. I have often wondered what it would have been like for those sitting in the Corinthian church hearing this letter being read. Maybe they were _mpted to wonder which category the person sitting next to them fitted into. 'Was she a drunkard?' 'Was he an adulterer?' But there would have been no point in asking, as Paul put the emphasis on the 'were'. We cannot make our churches pure by questioning everybody's past. We would exclude ourselves on that basis, for those who ask get asked! We just need to accept what Paul wrote next, *'but you were washed, but you were sanctified, but you were justified in the name of the Lord Jesus and by the Spirit of our God'*.

Now theologically that statement of Paul's is back to front, for technically justification comes before sanctification. Justification is what occurs when God looks at us and says, "You are legally acquitted. You no longer have to pay the price. You can step down from the dock and walk free from the court." We could personalise it and say that being justified means 'it is just as if I'd never sinned'. Those who speak Pidgin English in Papua New Guinea would put it even more simply, 'E-say-'im-all-right'. I love that. If God says you are all right, then you are truly justified.

Now, still speaking theologically, when we have been justified we need to be sanctified. We need to be set apart from sin and set apart for God. Sanctification is about holiness and purity. But in this list, Paul sets sanctification ahead of justification and puts washing before both. It is his way of being practical. If we have done things involving our bodies, as some at Corinth had, and these have left us feeling tainted, being told that we are legally acquitted might not remove the sense of uncleanness. We would need to feel that God has washed us and set us apart before it could fully dawn on us that all charges against us have been dismissed because He Himself has paid the price.

John the Baptist had a great ministry of washing. Having 'The Baptist' as one's title sounds exceedingly grand but he could have been called John the Dipper. At one time it was thought that New Testament Greek was a special sacred language until they found there were documents actually written in the same Greek describing household chores. The word for 'baptise' could be used when washing clothes. John wanted people to know that their sins could be washed away. His actions were designed to point them to the only One who could do that most effectively and he used Old Testament sacrificial language to declare Jesus as *the Lamb of God who takes away the sin of the world!*[25] He was quick to affirm that *'I indeed baptise you with water unto repentance, but He who is coming… will baptise you with the Holy Spirit and fire'*.[26]

---

[25] John 1:29.
[26] Matthew 3:11.

Nevertheless, John expected his followers to *'bear fruits worthy of repentance'*.[27] It was a good starting point, as our efforts to effect a change in the way we live prepare our hearts for God to truly purify us. Jesus gave clear directives for those who wish to demonstrate a commitment to change:

> *...whoever slaps you on the right cheek, turn the other to him also. If anyone wants to sue you and take away your tunic, let him have your cloak also. And whoever compels you to go one mile, go with him two.*[28]

We might need to see a shift in our attitude. There is no point saying we have repented if we are not demonstrating an intention to live differently. But our transformed actions have to stand alongside our faith in the only One who can truly transform us. If we fail to see good works in the context of faith, they end up being no more than self-promotion.[29]

John the Baptist's ministry ushered in a New Covenant. In the Old Testament every priest was ceremonially washed before being consecrated for sacred

---

[27] Matthew 3:8.

[28] Matthew 5:39-41.

[29] John 3:21.

service.[30] The washing we receive in Christ is even more thorough. Hebrews 10:19 says,

> *Therefore, brethren, having boldness to enter the Holiest by the blood of Jesus, by a new and living way which He consecrated for us, through the veil, that is, His flesh, and having a High Priest over the house of God, let us draw near with a true heart in full assurance of faith, having our hearts sprinkled from an evil conscience and our bodies washed with pure water.*

The conviction that is needed

We have seen how the Holy Spirit works in agreement with the blood and the cross, bringing forgiveness, cleansing and the restoration of relationships. We have seen too how the Holy Spirit works in agreement with the water and the word, securing the cutting-back of self-centredness and transforming us through the washing of regeneration and renewal. Before we pause at the close of the chapter for a moment of further reflection, we need to see how all of these things that open up a pathway to God's purity are in fact linked to the convicting work of the Holy Spirit.

[30] Leviticus 8:6.

On the night that Jesus was betrayed, He said of the Holy Spirit, *'when He has come, He will convict the world of sin, and of righteousness, and of judgment'*.[31] When the Holy Spirit begins to work in our lives we quickly become aware of our sin, and it is interesting that it is 'sin' of which He convicts, and not 'sins'. John the Baptist had people confessing their sins before he baptised them, publicly owning up to all they had done. They came out of the water able to claim that they had been cleansed, even though as yet they had no internal power beyond their own will-power to help them lead a new life. Helpfully, though, he told them that the *'the axe is laid to the root'*.[32] Repenting of our sins is rather like picking rotten apples off a tree one by one, knowing that there are a vast number of apples still to pick. The better solution is to have the axe laid to the root. The real work of the Holy Spirit in bringing us to repentance is not to make us list the things that we have done wrong but to make us realise that the list exists because we are wrong in ourselves. In the end it involves repenting of who we are. It is the 'I' that has grown up inside us that needs to be cut down. The Holy Spirit comes to make that possible. Romans 8:13 counsels us rightly, *'if by the Spirit you put to death the deeds of the body, you will live'*.

---

[31] John 16:8.
[32] Matthew 3:10.

Although repentance involves a major realignment, it can happen in an instant. In Cornelius's household, Peter was in the middle of his sermon when those listening began to speak in languages they had never learnt. In reporting back to the Jerusalem church, Peter said *'The Holy Spirit fell upon them, as upon us at the beginning'* and he went on to affirm confidently that God had granted them *'repentance to life'*.[33]

Some people seem to repent and repent and yet never get into newness of life. True repentance involves moving on. Those present in Cornelius's house neither shouted out nor sobbed; they just turned around on the inside in a way that God instantly recognised and honoured by giving them the Holy Spirit.

Later, when Peter was at the Jerusalem Council relating the same incident, he said *'God made no distinction… purifying their hearts by faith'*.[34] Faith and repentance went hand-in-hand. The Holy Spirit convicted them of their needs and in an instant *'the axe is laid to the root.'*[35] From then on they could have said with Paul *'It is no longer I who live, but Christ lives in me; and the life which I now live in the flesh I live by faith in the Son of God, who loved me and gave*

---

[33] Acts 11:15,18.

[34] Acts 15:9.

[35] Matthew 3:10.

Himself for me'.[36] It is this cutting back of self that sets us on the journey to securing God's purity.

And for further reflection…

In 1826 the English Congregationalist minister Thomas Binney wrote a hymn that expands on the theme of God dwelling in unapproachable light. I will share his words as a suitable conclusion to this chapter.

> **Eternal light, eternal light**
> **How pure the soul must be**
> **When placed within Thy searching sight,**
> **It shrinks not, but with pure delight,**
> **Can live and look on Thee.**
>
> **The spirits that surround Thy throne**
> **May bear the burning bliss;**
> **But that is surely theirs alone**
> **Since they have never, never known**
> **A fallen world like this.**
>
> **Oh, how shall I whose native sphere**
> **Is dark, whose mind is dim,**

---

[36] Galatians 2:20.

Before the ineffable appear,
And on my naked spirit bear
The uncreated beam?

There is a way for man to rise
To that sublime abode,
An offering and a sacrifice,
A Holy Spirit's energies,
An advocate with God.

These, these prepare us for the sight
Of holiness above;
The sons of ignorance and night,
May dwell in the eternal light
Through the eternal love.

3

Safeguarding our purity

Safeguarding our purity

Let us take 2 Corinthians 6:3-10 as our starting point:

We give no offense in anything, that our ministry may not be blamed. But in all things we commend ourselves as ministers of God: in much patience, in tribulations, in needs, in distresses, in stripes, in imprisonments, in tumults, in labours, in sleeplessness, in fastings; by purity, by knowledge, by longsuffering, by kindness, by the Holy Spirit, by sincere love, by the word of truth, by the power of God, by the armour of righteousness on the right hand and on the left, by honour and dishonour, by evil report and good report; as deceivers, and yet true; as unknown, and yet well known; as dying, and behold we live; as chastened, and yet not killed; as sorrowful, yet always rejoicing; as poor, yet making many rich; as having nothing, and yet possessing all things.

Paul certainly had a busy life and it is interesting that in the midst of his list of ministry challenges he mentions, *'by purity'*. Purity was important for Paul. All of us are in ministry in some way or another, facing ministerial challenges as we seek to serve God and those around us, so we have to behave aright, although the devil tries to bring us down.

And Paul knew what it meant to be brought low again and again, but not once could the devil claim to have ruled him out. Paul's secret was resurrection life. If we rise up every time the devil tries to bring us down, we will quickly discover that the greater the challenge, the greater the testimony. Paul could speak of stripes and imprisonments, tumults, labours, sleeplessness and fastings, then cite purity, knowledge, longsuffering, and sincere love as the essence of his ministerial survival methodology.

For Paul all of this was a serious matter. He even referred to disciplining his own body to bring it into subjection, lest *'when I have preached to others, I myself should become disqualified'*.[1] Now Paul had such confidence in his salvation that even the mention of disqualification sounds extraordinary. He knew that he had transferred from the kingdom of darkness to the kingdom of light, and that

---

[1] 1 Corinthians 9:27.

God had showered His grace and mercy on him.[2] Yet despite these certainties, he still had the determination to, in Peter's words, make his *'calling and election sure'*.[3]

Peter wrote that *'an entrance will be supplied to you abundantly into the everlasting kingdom'*, confirming that there is little point in aiming to enter heaven by the smallest possible margin.[4] The mentality that says, 'I'll just hope to scrape in!' is not good enough. Paul lived his life confident in the grace of God and in the salvation he knew he had received, and yet, at the same time, he wanted to do more. For him, salvation was not about feeling secure in himself but about bringing honour and glory to God.

It would be good if more of us shared Paul's commitment to protecting the ministry from blame. In the end it is not personal reputational risk that is the issue. In some ways, the more obsessed we are about our own reputations, the more we could be putting the ministry at risk. Jesus made Himself of no reputation so that He could serve everybody. When we are obsessed about our reputations, we can forget that ministry actually means serving. Preening ourselves as we sit on high counts for nothing. We should take the lowest place and do whatever it takes to build up others.

---

[2] Colossians 1:13; 1 Timothy 1:14.
[3] 2 Peter 1:10.
[4] 2 Peter 1:11.

So purity is important because impurity will bring our witness to Christ, as well as the Church and ministry in general, into disrepute. Incredible as it may sound, God has chosen to be seen in the light of his Church. In the book of Revelation, Jesus is shown walking in the midst of seven lampstands that represent two churches shining brightly and five with flickering flames on the verge of going out. To many of us this would appear to be the most inappropriate backdrop for the One who, at the start of His earthly ministry, described His followers as 'the light of the world'.[5] Even more embarrassing is the realisation that when Jesus spoke and John turned to see the voice, John saw the lampstands (the Church) even before he saw the One in their midst.[6] Such is the extent of God's commitment to us.

No-one can adopt a holier-than-thou attitude when reflecting on these things, since each of us is still a work-in-progress. We have to press forward, knowing that a threefold process is underway: we have been saved, we are being saved, and we will be saved. God's Spirit has become one with our spirit, so that we have passed from death to life. God is now renewing our minds, our wills and our emotions so that our souls are being reshaped by His grace. Eventually, He will renew our bodies, but until

---

[5] Matthew 5:14.
[6] Revelation 1:12,13.

that day the Spirit is giving life to our mortal bodies so that we can live in His fullness whilst awaiting that ultimate transformation. As John wrote in his first letter, *'it has not yet been revealed what we shall be, but we know that when He is revealed, we shall be like Him, for we shall see Him as He is'.*[7] It is incredible what God is going to do. *'We shall all be changed – in a moment, in the twinkling of an eye'.*[8]

In chapter 1 we looked at 'the source of purity' and our key words were light, life and love. In chapter 2 we looked at 'securing purity' and our key words were the blood, the water and the Spirit. As we now look at 'safeguarding purity', we will use three headings: 'a labour of love', 'a relationship of life' and 'alive in the light', focusing on our work, our walk and our worship.

A labour of love

The phrase *'labour of love'* occurs in Hebrews 6:10:

> **For God is not unjust to forget your work and labour of love which you have shown toward His name, in that you have ministered to the saints, and do minister.**

---

[7] 1 John 3:2.
[8] 1 Corinthians 15:51-52.

It is also found in 1 Thessalonians 1:2-4:

> *We give thanks to God always for you all, making mention of you in our prayers, remembering without ceasing your work of faith, labour of love, and patience of hope in our Lord Jesus Christ in the sight of our God and Father, knowing, beloved brethren, your election by God.*

I remember being quite shocked as a young Christian picking up Hallesby's book on prayer to discover that he had included a chapter on 'Prayer as Work'.[9] Initially the thought did not appeal to me, but I have since realised that we need to be workmanlike in praying if we are going to make a difference in the world, so rolling up our sleeves and putting in some effort is a must. But it is not just intercessory prayer that we need to work at. Paul obviously worked hard on his own life to make sure that he did not bring the ministry into disrepute. It is Paul's determination to discipline his body, despite his confidence in his calling, which leads us into this consideration of 'a labour of love'. We as Christians have things to work at!

Even when Hebrews 4:11 speaks of entering into rest, it says that we should be *'diligent to enter that rest'*, which seems strange as diligence implies effort. The reality is that

---

9   O. Hallesby, *'Prayer'*, IVF, London 1965.

the kind of rest God wants us to experience is a perfect rest where we come to peace, knowing we have attained all that God holds in His heart for us. It is not a casual kind of ease where we have given up on effort and have floated off into our dreams. God's rest is so important that we must make entering it a priority.

In the Galatian letter Paul contrasts the fruit of the Spirit with the works of the flesh, but that is not to imply that all the work we do automatically excludes the Holy Spirit. Working to enter God's rest definitely requires God's power, as well as God's purity, love and grace. However, some responsibility does come our way too if we are to know God's true peace and rest. Such responsibility is not the impossible responsibility of self-salvation, where we strive in the vain hope of being saved by our works. We know that we are saved by grace through faith. Even so, at the end of our lives God will be looking at our works to see if they were performed in faith. Everything we have done with Him will count for something and everything we have done without Him will count for nothing.

I used the expression 'counts for' deliberately, as people claim to live the whole of their lives without reference to God and yet appear to achieve a great deal.

But it was Jesus who said, *'without Me you can do nothing'.*[10] We all know that if we sit a test and answer questions that are not on the paper, our final score will be zero. There will not even be a consolation mark for spelling our name correctly. And that is precisely how God has set His test of a lifetime. It measures what we have done with Him and ignores what we have done without Him. The world might give us decorations but the only accolade worth having is God saying, *'Well done, good and faithful servant… Enter into the joy of the Lord'.*[11]

It may be helpful to allow John 3:20-21 to bring some further clarity on this:

> **Everyone practising evil hates the light and does not come to the light, lest his deeds should be exposed. But he who does the truth comes to the light, that his deeds may be clearly seen, that they have been done in God.**

Those who want their good deeds validated should come to the light and acknowledge God to be their source.[12]

But for many of us, the problem may be different. Before we were born again, we did not so much excel in

---

[10] John 15:5.

[11] Matthew 25:23.

[12] Matthew 5:16.

good works as in works of the flesh. Doing everything with a selfish motive just seemed to come naturally. No one had to coach us; we succeeded with ease. Now that we have had a change of nature, good works should come just as naturally. Ephesians 2:10 speaks of us as *'His workmanship, created in Christ Jesus for good works, which God prepared beforehand that we should walk in them'*. This has to be our goal, but it is all too easy to allow intensity or complacency to rob us of the reality. Intensity may have us seeking to serve others in a way that strives to gain approval to counter our all-too-often unacknowledged insecurities. Complacency may keep us from serving at all, leaving us at risk of slipping off into the roadside ditch just for want of walking in good works.

Psalm 119:9 gives some sound advice to young men that we would all do well to take hold of: *'How can a young man cleanse his way? By taking heed according to Your word'*. The message is clear, we need to take time to discover God's will and His ways in His word, then make the effort to apply them in our lives. This is exactly what Paul had in mind every time he took stock of himself after preaching to others. For Paul it was never a case of seeking to crucify the flesh by the flesh. Romans 8:13 tells us that *'if by the Spirit you put to death the deeds of the body, you will live'*. We need to remember that in taking up the cross daily we are only enforcing the reality that Christ's crucifixion has counted as ours from the day we first truly put our trust in Him.

There are those who find it easier to blame their problems with impurity on evil spirits, rather than recognise the role of their own fallen nature, but even after deliverance there needs to be a walk with the Deliverer. His counsel always needs heeding and His presence acts as a laser light, that not only exposes problem areas but can obliterate them too. However, walking in purity is not just about letting go of the old; we need to reach out with determination and take hold of the new. Paul gave the Romans the agenda and provided the Philippians with an action plan:

> *Do not be conformed to this world, but be transformed by the renewing of your mind, that you may prove what is that good and acceptable and perfect will of God.*[13]

> *Whatever things are true, whatever things are noble, whatever things are just, whatever things are pure, whatever things are lovely, whatever things are of good report, if there is any virtue and if there is anything praiseworthy – meditate on these things.*[14]

---

[13] Romans 12:2.
[14] Philippians 4:8.

So having already referred to Hebrews 12:14 and its emphasis on *'holiness, without which no one will see the Lord'*, we need to grapple with the expectation that it places on us. Clearly, if there are sin habits in our lives, they need to be broken. The first and most important step here is to receive God's forgiveness. There is a power in sin that stems from our readiness to hold on to dead works. We need to see every dead work cleansed from our consciences.[15]

Let me offer some advice. If you think that you can keep yourself from committing a sin by constantly reminding yourself of it, you are more likely to commit it than avoid it. That is why God wants to purge our conscience from dead works. He does not want us to keep remembering all that we once were and forever reminding ourselves of some past misdeed in the hope of preventing a repetition. A conscience with unhelpful fixations is not going to give an accurate reading. A tuning fork can be struck to give a clear note, but not if it has had an array of sticky objects attached to it. It has to be de-cluttered. We can praise God for the truth of Hebrews 9:14, *'how much more shall the blood of Christ, who through the eternal Spirit offered Himself without spot to God, cleanse your conscience from dead works to serve the living God?'*

---

[15]   Hebrews 9:14.

There is, of course, a verse that can stand alongside Hebrews 12:14 to bring a transformative hope to that *'holiness, without which no one will see the Lord'*. It is 1 John 3:1-3 with its affirmation that when we see the Lord we shall be like Him:

> **Behold what manner of love the Father has bestowed on us, that we should be called children of God! Therefore the world does not know us, because it did not know Him. Beloved, now are we children of God; and it is not yet being revealed what we shall be, but we know that when He is revealed, we shall be like Him, for we shall see Him as He is. And everyone who has this hope in Him purifies himself, just as He is pure.**

So, as part of our labour of love is to purify ourselves, keeping the hope of transformation alive in our hearts has to be a key aspect of such an endeavour. Having determinedly laid hold of God's forgiveness, we need to fix our eyes on the One who is to come, rejoicing in the fact that one day He will make us as pure as He is pure. Far from lulling us into complacency this will stir us up to make all the progress we can before He returns. Whatever the rewards He has for us, they will be for what we have done in our present bodies, not in anticipation of what we may do in the new bodies that are to come, *'For we must all appear before the judgment seat of Christ, that each one may receive the things done in the body, according to what he has done, whether good or bad'.*[16]

I love the down-to-earth approach to holiness that James presents to us in His letter. Paul's advice to the Philippians on purifying our thoughts was both practical and forthright; James wrote equally practically about purifying our words and deeds. Luther may have concluded that James' emphasis on works made him anti-faith, but in fact James was strong on faith, explaining that faith needs to be demonstrated through the way we live. When we read James we discover what it means to have our feet on the ground whilst holding to our Head (Christ) in the heavens.

Paul raised concerns about people around the church in Colossae who were close to cheating the church members out of their reward by:

> **taking delight in false humility and worship of angels, intruding into those things which he has not seen, vainly puffed up in his own fleshly mind, and not holding fast to the Head, from whom the**

---

[16] 2 Corinthians 5:10.

whole body, nourished and knit together by joints and ligaments, grows with the increase that is from God'.[17]

James is a good antidote for those today who have their head in the clouds and their feet off the ground, people who are in danger of losing contact with the realities of the Gospel and releasing their grip on the Lord. We need to labour to stay real, and if we have friends who are seeking to draw us off into unreality, we might be wise to avoid them until we have become stronger, strong enough to distract them from their distractions and bring them back on course.

We need to be careful, though, when speaking of those who see things differently from us. Paul's teaching on the mind and James's teaching on the tongue both need to be followed. Paul's counsel was to meditate on *'whatever things are of good report'*. As a young Christian I was told to 'talk nothing up but the Lord and talk nothing down but the devil'. When we are planning to bring a negative report, we need to pause and consider how to bring a positive one.

My wife is really good at helping me with this. A large part of my ministry over the years has involved opening

---

[17]   Colossians 2:18-19.

doors for others, and occasionally what they have carried with them as they have crossed the threshold has taken me by surprise. In the past I have been tempted to unburden myself the moment I reached home, but Marion would remind me that keeping our home as a haven is a greater blessing than compounding my negativity. Over the years her words have proved right. Negativity can cause us to lose touch with reality and constantly rehearsed negative reports can become riddled with fiction, carrying us and others into a fantasy world where self-righteousness mingles with discouragement.[18]

Perhaps it is for this reason that I have become suspicious of negative 'state of the nation' reports, whether delivered by residents or recent arrivals. Not long ago someone gave me an insight into the Wesleyan revival of the 1700s that included snapshots of Britain before and after. It was a story of transformation that would make salutary reading for those who talk as if Britain now is at its worst, and devoid of the possibility of resuscitation. We need to celebrate evidences for hope rather than search out causes for dismay. It should not be hard to see the positives around and surely focusing our minds and taming our tongues are labours worth pursuing.

---

[18]   Luke 24:13-17, 31-32.

James asks his readers a rhetorical question, '*Does a spring send forth fresh water and bitter from the same opening?*'[19] In answering 'no', as the text requires, we are endorsing James' preceding explanation, '*My brethren, these things ought not to be so*'.[20] For James, an unchecked tongue is not only an unreliable spring but an incendiary device, or an unhelpful rudder.[21] We must demonstrate our faith by checking our tongue, extinguishing its fires, sweetening its words and rightly steering our lives. At the same time, we need to accept that empty words can be just as malicious as duplicitous ones. If we have faith for provision, then pious pronouncements, such as 'be blessed, be warmed, be filled', have to be supported by genuine care in action.[22]

Words and deeds go hand-in-hand. We are exhorted to be '*doers of the word, and not hearers only, deceiving yourselves*'.[23] James describes God's word as '*the perfect law of liberty*'. Those who fail to apply what they see in it are like an unkempt character who on '*observing his natural face in a mirror… goes away, and immediately forgets what kind of man he was*'.[24] We must look long enough and hard enough to identify our shortcomings, then take the time and trouble

---

[19] James 3:11.
[20] James 3:10.
[21] James 3:1-10.
[22] James 2:14-16.
[23] James 1:22.
[24] James 1:24-25.

to present God's intended image to the world, a task that requires continual inward transformation:

> *'Therefore lay aside all filthiness and overflow of wickedness, and receive with meekness the implanted word, which is able to save your souls.'*[25]

To conclude these thoughts on a labour of love, we will return to one of Paul's illustrations, that of a race. We cannot be apathetic when preparing for a race. We need to be spiritually fit and strong in faith as we plan for victory. Most of us run faster when there is someone setting the pace for us so it would be foolish to be self-centred in our preparations. We will never be running alone, so when the writer to the Hebrews encourages us to *'consider one another in order to stir up love and good works'* we should welcome the opportunity to spur each other on.[26]

Paul wrote to Timothy, *'flee… youthful lusts'* and taking flight certainly increases our fitness to race.[27] If we are serious about safeguarding purity, we will run hard whenever impurity is on offer. It is better to run off at a pace than to stay around and be overwhelmed by temptation. Fleeing lust is as much a part of running the race as is reaching the finishing tape.

---

[25] James 1:21.
[26] Hebrews 10:24.
[27] 2 Timothy 2:22.

When the writer to the Hebrews affirms the need to lay sin aside, some of us may be emboldened by the fact that he writes of *'the sin which so easily ensnares us'*.[28] Of course, all sin is a snare, but there is no doubt that the devil seeks to tie particular sins to particular people, leaving them thinking that their personal problems have a grip on them that is unbreakable. We need to take heart from the context of the exhortation to the Hebrews:

> **Therefore we also, since we are surrounded by so great a cloud of witnesses, let us lay aside every weight, and the sin which so easily ensnares us, and let us run with endurance the race that is set before us, looking unto Jesus, the author and finisher of our faith, who for the joy that was set before Him endured the cross, despising the shame, and has sat down at the right hand of the throne of God.**[29]

This whole chapter is an encouragement. No matter how strongly sin ensnares us, God's forgiveness can break the link. The psalmist declares rightly, *'As far as the east is from the west, so far has He removed our transgressions from us'*.[30] Sin can be laid aside and so can every weight. We have the power of God, the example of Christ, and a host of witnesses who have overcome before us.

---

[28] Hebrews 12:1.

[29] Hebrews 12:1-2.

[30] Psalm 103:12.

'Weights' are those legitimate pursuits and responsibilities that can slow us down in the race. Paul wrote *'All things are lawful for me, but not all things are helpful'.*[31] Different things can be a hindrance at different times in our lives. It was reassuring some years ago when someone kindly sought to encourage me by saying that 'everything you have ever done is going to be used by God'. What caught my attention was that he then went on to list things such as academic study, writing, and inter-denominational engagement, all of which I had at some point laid aside. I had no regrets, though, over having run without them, even when I was thinking that God might be asking me to do so permanently rather than for a season. I am sure that constantly trying to handle them alongside other more immediate assignments would only have slowed me down in my efforts to be effective for God.

We have to remember that God is not trying to impoverish us when exhorting us to remove every hindrance from our lives. When Jesus told the rich young ruler to give all his wealth to the poor, He was helping to lift a weight off his life.[32] Thinking back, I remember a conference speaker saying 'imagine trying to run a race with a grand piano strapped to your back'. At the time that was hard for me to hear as I was looking for a really

---

[31] 1 Corinthians 10:23.
[32] Matthew 19:21; Mark 10:21; Luke 18:22.

good keyboard. I realised, though, that doing without one would be a small sacrifice compared with the sacrifices of those who have given up all for the Lord. Sometimes in later life God replenishes us with far more than we set aside. Many years later I had the liberty to buy the piano. But I know that if anything that has once hindered should ever start to hinder again, it would be better to go without for a second time in order to prioritise spiritual progress.

If we leave something at the start line of a race, be it a broken sin habit or a discarded weight, we must run with confidence and stop imagining it is still pursuing us. Athletes who lay their track suits down before they run do not look round during the race to see if their clothes are chasing them down the track. And we need to think twice too about the fears some of us have over the devil. The Bible says, *'resist the devil and he will flee from you'*.[33] It is good to know that it does not say 'resist the devil and he will fly at you'. If we are resisting the devil and fleeing lusts, the gap is widening, not closing.

Another lesson to bear in mind is that the devil misquotes Scripture and uses it selectively. When he was tempting Jesus, he set Jesus in a precarious position on the pinnacle of the temple.[34] Now the Bible says of Jesus that,

---

[33] James 4:7.
[34] Luke 4:9.

'we do not have a High Priest who cannot sympathise with our weaknesses, but was in all points tempted as we are, yet without sin'.[35] Some of us, however, panic whenever the devil puts us in a precarious position, and then fall because we think that being poised precariously means we must already have sinned. Jesus did not fall, nor launch Himself off at the devil's invitation. Jesus knew that when the devil was quoting Psalm 91:11-12, *'For He shall give His angels charge over you, to keep you in all your ways. In their hands they shall bear you up, lest you dash your foot against a stone'*, he was stopping short of verse 13: *'You shall tread upon the lion and the cobra, the young lion and the serpent you shall trample underfoot'*. We too need to become fully conversant with the Bible and emulate those in Corinth who, according to Paul, were not ignorant of the devil's devices.[36] Romans 16:20 holds out a great promise to us all, *'And the God of peace will crush Satan under your feet shortly'*.

Maybe a story will help underscore the importance of not being intimidated when we find ourselves in a precarious position. Someone I know immediately rang a friend when a lady he had never met before gave him a smile at the gym. He simply explained over the phone what had happened and asked his friend to pray that, if

---

[35] Hebrews 4:15.

[36] 2 Corinthians 2:11.

she smiled again, he would not find himself compromised. I have no way of knowing what lay behind that smile but I am glad that someone was taking no risks. Too many of us have seen friends fall, maybe for want of a telephone call.

Perhaps a more general word about physical attraction would not go amiss. Sometimes married couples, and this was not the case behind the story I have just mentioned, find that the things that initially attracted them to each other lose their lustre. This normally means it is time to look again in the original direction rather than to start looking elsewhere. God can help you rediscover that initial sense of attraction, no matter what others may be trying to tell you. And who knows, you may find areas of attractiveness in one another that you missed first time around! Some people lose their marriages because their labour of love stops short of labouring for love.

So far we have said more about the things we are to flee than the things we are to pursue. We need to remind ourselves of both sides of the dual encouragement that Paul gave Timothy: *'Flee also youthful lusts; but pursue righteousness, faith, love, peace with those who call on the Lord out of a pure heart'*.[37] Paul was not alone in linking love and a pure heart, as Peter did the same when he wrote *'Love one*

---

[37] 2 Timothy 2:22.

another fervently with a pure heart'.[38] This counsel is given to us as a safeguard, maximising the security that living our lives in the context of Christian fellowship is intended to provide. Even so, it is no small challenge as 'fervently' implies 'at full stretch'.[39] Some of us can remember how well we began, agreeing with 1 John 3:14, *'We know that we have passed from death to life, because we love the brethren'*. Perhaps we now need to stretch ourselves again to love those we once loved at full stretch before our love contracted. Many of us may know the little rhyme:

> **To live above with saints we love...**
> **Ah, that will be the glory.**
> **To live below with saints we know...**
> **Well, that's a different story.**

But it should not be like that. Living below with saints we know should also be glory, and it can be. We just have to love one another fervently out of a pure heart.

There is some useful imagery in 2 Timothy 2:20-21. To fully appreciate it, we need to see ourselves among the many varied vessels in a great house, all aspiring to be useful to the master:

---

[38] 1 Peter 1:22.
[39] Greek εκτενως (*ek*, out, *teino*, stretch).

...in a great house there are not only vessels of gold and silver, but also of wood and clay, some for honour and some for dishonour. Therefore if anyone cleanses himself from the latter, he will be a vessel for honour, sanctified and useful for the Master, prepared for every good work.

It is not about whether we are wood, gold, clay or silver. The only questions are 'Have we been cleansed?' and 'Are we useable?' Clay pots can be as useful as gold goblets but gold goblets that remain un-cleansed have to be set aside. We have to respect the work God is doing in each of our lives and set our faces towards purity. It may not surprise you to hear me say that cleansing ourselves and loving each other are labours of love that have to be pursued.

A relationship of life

Now alongside the labour of love, there needs to be a relationship of life, or in other words, a walk in the Spirit. Romans 8:1 reminds us that, *'There is therefore now no condemnation to those who are in Christ Jesus, who do not walk according to the flesh, but according to the Spirit'*. Galatians 5:16 emphasises the same point: *'Walk in the Spirit, and you shall not fulfil the lust of the flesh'*.

Paul also makes a distinction between the leading of the Spirit and the limitation of the law, *'if you are led by the Spirit, you are not under the law'*.[40] He then reinforces this, after listing the fruit of the Spirit, by adding the words *'Against such there is no law'*.[41] The fact that there is no law against the fruit of the Spirit means that there is no legal limit to the work God can do in our lives as we continue to walk with Him. We can see a strengthening of our dependence on the Holy Spirit and a resultant increase in fruitfulness, even as we see a crucifying of the flesh and an ending of its works:

> *But the fruit of the Spirit is love, joy, peace, longsuffering, kindness, goodness, faithfulness, gentleness, self-control. Against such there is no law. And those who are Christ's have crucified the flesh with its passions and desires. If we live in the Spirit, let us also walk in the Spirit.*[42]

All the time we are 'walking in the Spirit', prioritising our life with God, we are becoming less dependent upon our strong-mindedness, wilfulness and self-orientated emotions. Not surprisingly, if we determine not to 'walk in the flesh', the less likely we will be to have works of the

---

[40] Galatians 5:18.

[41] Galatians 5:23.

[42] Galatians 5:22-25.

flesh dominating our lives. A somewhat over-simplistic example may help to illustrate the point. If we live for flattery, rather than walking humbly with God, people's ingratiating words will soon become everything to us and we will quickly become prey to anyone who offers us the smallest degree of admiration. It is a slippery slope. Rather than crucifying the flesh we will end up encouraging it. It is better by far to walk in the Spirit. That way we will see through the flattery and not succumb to it.

Each of the other works of the flesh could furnish their own backstories to make the same point. It is quite a list: *'adultery, fornication, uncleanness, lewdness, idolatry, sorcery, hatred, contentions, jealousies, outbursts of wrath, selfish ambitions, dissensions, heresies, envy, murders, drunkenness, revelries, and the like'* — a real reminder to safeguard purity in our lives by walking in the Spirit.[43]

Not only is it true that *'the Spirit Himself bears witness with our spirit that we are children of God'* but we can affirm to one another that *'He who raised Christ from the dead will also give life to your mortal bodies through His Spirit who dwells in you'*.[44] It is a totally transforming relationship. As we walk in the Spirit, the Holy Spirit is able to continually pour His

---

[43] Galatians 5:19-21.
[44] Romans 8:16 and 11.

life into our lives. This is how God fulfils Paul's prayer for
the Thessalonians:

> **Now may the God of peace Himself sanctify you
> completely; and may your whole spirit, soul, and
> body be preserved blameless at the coming of our
> Lord Jesus Christ.**[45]

At the same time, the fruitfulness of the Spirit is expressed
in our lives through an ever-increasing supply of God's
*'love, joy, peace, longsuffering, kindness, goodness, faithfulness,
gentleness, self-control'.*[46]

James presents us with a similar picture of
transformation when he speaks of the wisdom from above
as being *'first pure, then peaceable, gentle, willing to yield,
full of mercy and good fruits, without partiality and without
hypocrisy'.*[47] He then adds *'Now the fruit of righteousness is
sown in peace by those who make peace'.*[48] Here the contrast is
with the wisdom that James describes as earthly, sensual
and demonic':

> **But if you have bitter envy and self-seeking in your
> hearts, do not boast and lie against the truth. This
> wisdom does not descend from above, but is earthly,**

---

[45]   1 Thessalonians 5:23.
[46]   Galatians 5:22-23.
[47]   James 3:17.
[48]   James 3:18.

sensual, demonic. For where envy and self-seeking exist, confusion and every evil thing are there.[49]

There is a clear link between the wisdom that is from above and the fruit of the Spirit.

James says that *'the wisdom that is from above is first pure'*. God, whose wisdom has been exemplified among us in the purity of Christ, now brings that wisdom to us through the power of His Spirit. In a world where all too often selfish ambition is the path to promotion, God promotes a wisdom that can rise to the fore in any debate because of its unselfconscious integrity.

Furthermore, with strident competitiveness removed from our agenda, we discover that the wisdom from above is peaceable, gentle and willing to yield. This indeed is a rare wisdom in a day when any apparent preparedness to back down is suspected as a negotiating ploy for gaining tactical advantage. And a wisdom that is *'full of mercy and good fruits, without partiality and without hypocrisy'*, is definitely worth asking for. We can be grateful that James assures us that *'if any of you lacks wisdom, let him ask of God, who gives to all liberally and without reproach, and it will be given him'*.[50]

---

[49] James 3:14-16.
[50] James 1:5.

Now of course humility is essential if we are to walk in a relationship of life with the Holy Spirit, and there are two scripture verses that I find particularly helpful. The first is Philippians 2:3:

> *Let nothing be done through selfish ambition or conceit, but in lowliness of mind let each esteem others better than himself.*

We have seen this within the Godhead, where esteem is given and received without either denigration or pride, setting us the ultimate example. The second is Romans 12:3:

> *For I say, through the grace given to me, to everyone who is among you, not to think of himself more highly than he ought to think, but to think soberly, as God has dealt to each one a measure of faith.*

I remember one occasion when someone assured me that they had never thought more highly of themselves than they ought to have done. I considered it such an unusual statement that I asked, "Is it possible that you think of yourself more *often* than you ought to think?" At that point the message got across. It is possible to be self-obsessed even whilst we are trying to promote our self-abasement. Unfortunately, an inferiority complex can be just as complex and self-centred as a superiority complex. God wants to set us free from all self-obsession.

I know that some people get caught as they seek to rise to the challenge of loving their neighbour as themselves.[51] There was a time when some well-intentioned counsellors would urge us to ask ourselves 'Do I love myself enough?' This, of course, was never the right question. The issue at the heart of the Good Samaritan story is 'Am I loving myself more than I am loving my neighbour?' A more useful point to ponder would be the new commandment that Jesus gave us: *'A new commandment I give to you, that you love one another; as I have loved you'*.[52] It is far more profitable, humbling and affirming to reflect on how much love the Lord Jesus has for each one of us personally and then to build our lives and relationships based on that.

Of course, it is equally important to remember how much love God has for those He is commanding us to love. I constantly come back to Romans 14:4 as a standard: *'Who are you to judge another's servant? To his own master he stands or falls. Indeed, he will be made to stand, for God is able to make him stand'*. As a fellow servant with those who are yielding their lives to Christ, I must trust in the supportive grace our Master shows to each one of us.

---

[51] Luke 10:27.
[52] John 13:34.

God can do amazing things with the most unlikely people. That is why He chose you and me. He chooses *'the things which are not, to bring to nothing the things that are'*.[53] If we once thought that we were something, God found a way of making us realise that we were nothing in order to bring us to Himself in a right spirit. He may even have used someone whom we once despised to help us gain that necessary perspective.

Alive in the light

As we draw together our thoughts on safeguarding purity, 1 John 1:1 – 2:2 can help us grasp what it means to be 'alive in the light'. It will also help us conclude on a note of prayerful worship. I will quote the whole chapter:

> *That which was from the beginning, which we have heard, which we have seen with our eyes, which we have looked upon, and our hands have handled, concerning the Word of life — the life was manifested, and we have seen, and bear witness, and declare to you that eternal life which was with the Father and was manifested to us — that which we have seen and heard we declare to you, that you also may have fellowship with us; and truly our*

---

[53]   1 Corinthians 1:28.

fellowship is with the Father and with His Son Jesus Christ. And these things we write to you that your joy may be full.

This is the message which we have heard from Him and declare to you, that God is light and in him is no darkness at all. If we say that we have fellowship with Him, and walk in darkness, we lie and do not practise the truth. But if we walk in the light as He is in the light, we have fellowship with one another, and the blood of Jesus Christ His Son cleanses us from all sin. If we say we have no sin, we deceive ourselves, and the truth is not in us. If we confess our sins, He is faithful and just to forgive us our sins and to cleanse us from all unrighteousness. If we say that we have not sinned, we make him a liar, and His word is not in us. My little children, these things I write to you, that you may not sin. And if anyone sins, we have an Advocate with the Father, Jesus Christ the righteous. And he Himself is the propitiation for our sins, and not for ours only but also for the whole world.

These verses offer us a further glimpse into how God brings His purity to us. John focuses on the manifestation of God's life and light and the need for us to be bound together by love, not only with one another, but also with the Father and the Son, through the Holy Spirit. Practical experience teaches us that it is only clean surfaces that can be joined and it is the blood of Jesus that prepares us for such a union and enables us to sustain the level of fellowship that such unity affords.

In addition to this, though, we have Jesus speaking up for us as our Advocate. In Ephesians we are told that God the Father has:

> *...blessed us with every spiritual blessing in the heavenly places in Christ, just as He chose us in Him before the foundation of the world, that we should be holy and without blame before Him in love.*[54]

The word used for 'blessing' here could be translated 'well speaking' and the One who is doing the 'well speaking' on your behalf and mine is the Lord Jesus, who always lives to make intercession for us.[55] Right now we have a Defence Lawyer, an Advocate, in heaven. No wonder Paul was able to write to the Romans:

> *Who shall bring a charge against God's elect? It is God who justifies. Who is he who condemns? It is Christ who died, and furthermore is also risen, who*

[54] Ephesians 1:3-4.
[55] Hebrews 7:25.

is even at the right hand of God, who also makes intercession for us.[56]

In safeguarding our purity, Jesus will always tell the truth — how could He do otherwise as He not only dwells in unapproachable light, but is that light? There is, however, one who seeks to sully us with negative words, haranguing us with endless discouragements designed to make us lose hope and fall into compromise. The good news is that, whilst we battle with that accuser's unfounded negative words on earth, there is One who will always be countering them where it really matters. This alone should cause us to lift our hearts in worship.

It is a tremendous privilege to be 'alive in the light' and God must receive all the glory for purifying us. Without the power of His purity we could never be in His presence. It is good that our transformation is so unmerited that none of us will be distracted by it in that ultimate place of worship. Even the crowns that we may receive are for casting before Him.[57] In the midst of our fullness of joy, we will be totally focused on His spotless glory.[58]

For now, we cannot see everything that we will see, but God is working in our hearts and lives, and His purity

---

[56] Romans 8:33-34.
[57] Revelation 4:10.
[58] Psalm 16:11.

is beginning to be expressed among us. As the blood of Jesus cleanses us, and the word of God washes us, we can walk in the light, knowing what it is to have the Holy Spirit convicting us of sin, of righteousness and of judgment. And although there is far more of God's light, life and love for us to comprehend, we are able to rejoice in all that we have received, labouring in love, walking in life and worshipping in the light.

I began this book by saying that I hope my chosen title has not attracted those just out to impress their friends or dazzle their detractors. Whatever your original expectations, though, I trust that you have caught a glimpse of the purity of God, and have realised that God is doing everything to make that purity available to each one of us. We are not getting it cheaply because Jesus has paid a great price and we need to respect that by walking in daily partnership with the Holy Spirit.

There are so many scriptures with which I could end this book and I was particularly drawn to the reference to the highway of holiness in Isaiah 35:8-10. In the end, however, I have opted for Ezekiel 36, as it holds us to the basics, even whilst opening up for us the greatest of heights. There are echoes of the account in Acts 10, where Peter's message was interrupted by the coming of the Holy

Spirit to those in Cornelius's household. In Peter's two subsequent reports of the event we read that *'God granted to the Gentiles repentance to life'* and that He *'made no distinction between us and them, purifying their hearts by faith'.*[59]

So as we read God's words in Ezekiel 36:26, given to a nation that had His laws inscribed on tablets of stone, let us see how today we can have these very means of attaining God's perfection and purity written on our renewed and responsive hearts, ready to be fulfilled in us and through us by the power of the Holy Spirit:

> *I will give you a new heart and put a new spirit within you; I will take the heart of stone out of*
>
> *your flesh and give you a heart of flesh. I will put my spirit within you and cause you to walk in my statutes, and you will keep my judgments and do them.*

---

[59] Acts 11:18; 15:9.

A prayer

Father, I thank You, for the reality of a heart made new. Thank You for taking away my heart of stone, with its pride, arrogance and self-centredness, which made me so resistant to You.

Thank You for giving me a responsive heart on which You have written Your laws, laws that no longer hang over me in judgment, but living words for me to fulfil in the power of Your Spirit.

Lord, I thank You for all You are doing in these days to enable Your people to bring a good report. Thank You for the many fresh stirrings there are in Your Church, even as we hunger for more of You.

Lord, I ask You to bring yet greater revelations of Your purity before my eyes and use them to help me discover more of Your light, love and life, so that I can better reflect Your glory, and bring honour to Your name.

In Jesus' name I pray. Amen.

Thank you for reading.

For more teaching materials from
Hugh Osgood do visit the website

*

ALL IN-DEPTH BIBLE TEACHING SERIES
...TOTALLY FREE TO DOWNLOAD

UPCOMING EVENTS AND CONFERENCES

MINISTRY UPDATES AND REPORTS

COURSES WITH 'HUGH OSGOOD ACADEMICS'

*

WWW.HUGHOSGOOD.COM

Stay up-to-date with
Hugh Osgood's ministry
by following on
Facebook, Twitter and YouTube

HUGH OSGOOD

@HUGHOSGOOD

HUGHOSGOOD

You can also support Hugh Osgood's ministry
by donating safely and securely online

WWW.HUGHOSGOOD.COM/DONATE